NEWMAN:
A Religious Quest

THOMAS O'LOUGHLIN

VERITAS

First published 1988 by
Veritas Publications
7/8 Lower Abbey Street
Dublin 1
Ireland

This revised edition published 2001

Email publications@veritas.ie
Website www.veritas.ie

ISBN 1 85390 553 4

Cover Photograph of Cardinal Newman taken in 1885 by Louis Barraud

Designed by Colette Dower
Printed in the Republic of Ireland by Betaprint Ltd, Dublin

Veritas books are printed on paper made from the wood pulp of managed forests. For every tree felled, at least one tree is planted, thereby renewing natural resources.

NEWMAN:
A Religious Quest

Different Worlds

It is just two centuries since John Henry Newman was born, and yet it is a foreign world. In France, Napoleon had just become Emperor and was at the height of his power; in the British Isles, the Act of Union had just been passed giving Westminster direct control over Irish affairs; and though the steam engine existed, the railway and the steamship were still decades away. It is just over a century since he died in what was recognisably the modern world: a world of industry, vast urban populations, mass communications, and a sense that somehow people were living in 'modern times' and that what was accepted in the past would no longer do. Straddling these two worlds is this curious Englishman whose life saw more changes than most, who proclaimed that to be alive is to be involved in change and that change was to be welcomed as offering the possibility of growth, yet who was convinced that there was a thread running through his life giving it constancy and consistency. Here lies the enigma of Newman; scholar, cleric, theologian, and saint. It is this enigma that accounts for the fact that he is probably the only Victorian clergyman who excites popular interest today. As soon as the name 'Newman' is mentioned, people who would otherwise ignore long dead priests sit up with interest. For some he is the great theologian whose writings continually surprise one in the way they throw new light on old problems. For others he is the great convert, or the great ecumenist, or indeed a saint for our time and is looked up to accordingly. For many more he is the author of the hymn 'Lead, kindly light' and of the poem 'The Dream of Gerontius'. Many are just curious since they know that he began his adult life as an Anglican priest and that when he died he was one of the cardinals of the Roman Church.

Newman is also important because of when he lived. He grew up during the Napoleonic Wars — he could remember the celebrations after Nelson defeated the French and Spanish navies at Trafalgar in 1805 — and during his long life he saw the modern world develop. He saw the growth of those ideas in science, politics, philosophy and about the nature and end of human beings that have been dominant ever since. It was during his life-time that the modern challenges to faith, and modern unbelief, arose. To all these developments he sought to pose questions: Are they true? Are they compatible with Christianity? How can faith live and grow in such a world? For this reason alone — his attempt to grapple with the links between faith and the modern world — his work is an important guide for us.

Beneath these reasons I suspect there is also a deeper attraction: in some unclear way we sense that he is an example of someone who, throughout his life, ignoring the cost, engaged in a fundamental human activity, the search for truth. In him there is the attraction of someone who changes a great deal over the years, and yet in his desires and aims hardly at all. It is because he did not change in the goals he pursued, that he had to change so much. From his teenage years Newman had a sense that he had to follow the light that God gave him, and so the externals of life had to be accommodated to that divine call. The ups and downs of his life, showing at once his humanity and his holiness, attract us. In this he stands in contrast to so many saints whose lives were models of stability — presented as a virtue — or who were sheltered from the changing world around them. For us who live in a world of rapid change where permanence is the exception, there is something attractive in someone whose pursuit of holiness involved so much disruption and so many changes in direction, who had the courage to strike out in new directions despite the objections of those around him.

THE NEWMANS

On 21 February 1801, John Henry Newman was born in London. He was the eldest of six children. His father, John, was a banker and the family were comfortably off. They were a very close, happy family and from the start the eldest appears to have been the apple of his parents' eye. As regards religion, they were in no way out of the ordinary. John Henry's father took religion lightly, and though his mother took it more seriously, religion was centred on bible-reading (done in quantities, and understood literally) and having an acceptable code of conduct. They were typical of a middle class that, despite financial ups and downs, would become the backbone of Victorian society. If, today, we wanted to imagine the culture in which John Henry grew up, then possibly our best guide is to imagine the world we see portrayed in the novels of Jane Austen.

The six children who grew up in this close, loving family would diverge as much as any family could. Mary, the youngest, born in 1809, died in 1828. The other girls, Harriet and Jemima, both married Anglican clergy and strongly disapproved when their brother became a Catholic; Harriet severing contact with him abruptly, Jemima losing touch over a period of time. His brother Frank, having gone through several extreme Protestant sects, eventually became a successful professor and died a convinced atheist. Charles, the youngest son, having failed to apply himself to either study or business, became a drifter living off whatever he could get from the family or elsewhere. Like Frank, he became an atheist.

Off to School

In 1808, aged seven, John Henry was sent to boarding school in Ealing. Slightly younger than the rest of his class, he nonetheless was able to keep pace with them and was remembered later as cheerful, witty and quite brilliant. His schooling was the standard fare of the time, first reading and writing, then maths and the classics. It was aimed at giving the student a fluency in reading and writing Latin and Greek, with a good knowledge of the Roman authors, and so enabling them to go to university or enter the professions. This taste for the classics remained with him; in later life he used to examine a sentence from a classical author each day as a way of keeping an edge on his written style. Newman began his life as a writer at this time. He began a school magazine called *The Spy*, and then, so that there could be controversy and competition, he also founded *The Counter-Spy*. This editorial skill (as well as the trick of controversy) would stand him in good stead. Also at this time we see the start of his lifelong habit of careful reflection and soul-searching in that he began to keep a personal diary.

In March 1816, the bank that was run by John Henry's father, John Newman, collapsed financially so that the family were in tight straits with regard to money. Being middle-class, they imagined themselves on the very brink of poverty. The ensuing crisis at home affected John Henry, to the extent that he became ill in the summer and had to remain at school for the holidays. There he came under the influence of the Rev. Walter Mayers. For someone like Newman coming from an Evangelical background, the Calvinism of Mayers would not have seemed that strange.

Through conversation and books a gradual change came over Newman. Later he called this his 'conversion'. It was the time when he began to take religion seriously, indeed to see the service of God as his life's task. The experience taught him several things. First, it was not enough just to do good, and avoid harming others; one must be 'religious and not merely ethical', i.e., one must actually practise a religion. Second, he gained a profound sense of the importance of revelation within Christianity: the beliefs involved in Christian faith were not just optional abstractions, but truths about life and salvation demanding acceptance. Third, he developed a love for the study of the early Christian saints and theologians (known as 'the Fathers of the Church') whom he imagined belonged to the pristine state of Christianity. And fourth, the strange combination of a belief that he was called to a celibate life, coupled with a deep abhorrence of everything connected with the Roman Catholic

Church. As Newman said later, he emerged from that summer a different person.

UP TO OXFORD

A few months after his conversion, Newman entered Trinity College, Oxford. He worked hard, winning in 1818 a scholarship for nine years worth £60 a year. Indeed he worked so hard, but without proper discipline, that when he sat his BA exams in November 1820 he got only a slightly above average mark. He read too widely, becoming so over-tired that he became ill during the exams. His studies, standard for Oxford at the time, centred on maths and classics. He emerged from his BA with a very definite love of Oxford, and certain that a clerical and academic life was for him.

FELLOW OF ORIEL

Newman remembered 12 April 1822 for the rest of his life as his happiest day: on that day he was elected a Fellow of Oriel College. Oriel was intellectually and religiously the most active of Oxford's colleges; to hold a position in it was no mean distinction. For Newman it was a turning point in many ways: intellectually it set him up for a life in the university and a life of wide influence; religiously it forged the man we now remember.

He came to it a rather gawkish youth who as an Evangelical believed that Christian faith was based solely on the Bible, and who distrusted and disliked any rational reflection or exploration of belief. Reason and thinking belonged to this world, while faith and believing belonged to another, and the two should not be mixed. In another college this fundamentalism would not have been challenged, but in Oriel he became friends with brilliant theologians who challenged him to drop many of his Evangelical attitudes and to understand more deeply the core of his faith which he retained.

A clergyman named Richard Whately, the most influential of the group, helped him most. He taught Newman how to think accurately and with purpose. Despite learning much from him, Newman would never accept Whately's liberal dislike for fixed doctrines. Nonetheless, Newman was thanked by Whately in the preface to his textbook on logic (published in 1826) thus: 'But I cannot avoid particularizing [for thanks] the Rev. J. Newman, Fellow of Oriel College, who actually composed a considerable portion of the work . . . from [my notes], and who is the original author of several pages.' Many ideas on human rationality that Newman learned from Whately at this time would appear in developed form in his *Grammar of Assent* in 1870.

Furthermore, Whately taught him the importance of the Church: a visible body moving through history that carries on God's work of salvation. Christian faith was not founded on a sacred book ('The Bible') but in the community, which was bound to Jesus Christ in baptism and discipleship, and which expressed that discipleship in many ways, such as in the writings that make up the Bible. Up to this time Newman held that the Church was just a collection of individuals and, since it was a 'club', he saw no reason why the state should not rule it as it regulated other groups within society. Through Whately he came to see it as a sacred edifice founded by God and ruled by the successors of the apostles. At a practical level, Whately promoted him within the university and helped him to get his first work published.

Friendships, often very close and long-standing, are a feature of Newman's life. He attracted friendship and disliked not having friends with whom he could communicate. At Oriel he made many friends and learned from all of them. One of those friendships was with Edward Bouverie Pusey (1800–92), elected Fellow on the same day as Newman. From him he learned the importance of tradition in Christianity. Another friendship began in 1826 when he became Tutor and was joined by the very Catholic-minded Hurrell Froude. Hurrell Froude held that to see Christianity really at work it was useless to look at the early centuries of the Church. For Froude, when one looked at the first centuries, one saw Christians who were a hidden minority. To really see Christianity, you had to look at it when it had transformed a society and was a

13

fully active force. You had to look to the Middle Ages and what you saw there, of course, looked very like the Roman Church! In this attitude Hurrell Froude was markedly different from most non-Catholic thinkers at the time, for whom the 'Middle Ages' were the 'Dark Ages of Romish superstition'. Newman was confident that such ideas as Froude's were ludicrous; after all, the Roman Church was encrusted with cancerous growths and, as had often been pointed out in Evangelical circles, it was 'the whore of Babylon' mentioned in Revelation 17:5.

On 13 June 1824 Newman was ordained a deacon in the Church of England and made curate in an Oxford church; and on 29 May 1825, he was ordained a priest. He noted that from then on he believed his life was to be given solely to the service of God. Three years later (1828) he became Vicar of St Mary's, the university church, and he proved himself to be a dedicated pastor. It was noted, for example, that he visited all the poor in his parish — and this was something he had to do alongside his academic work.

This pastoral concern soon got him into trouble, and into the first of many scrapes with ecclesiastical authorities that would dog his life down to 1879 when he was made a cardinal. Already he was exercising an enormous influence on undergraduates through his sermons in the university church: now, with Hurrell Froude, he felt that his duties to the students to whom he was tutor extended beyond their academic welfare. He believed he had a duty to help the students mature as Christian gentlemen. The Provost did not agree. Due to these differences of view on the range of his duties, Newman had to resign his tutorship in 1830. Thereafter he had no teaching office in the university.

Newman now spent his time on his sermons (he was one of the 'University Preachers' in 1831–2) and on his first book, *The Arians of the Fourth Century*, on the subject of heresy in the early Church. When published in 1833 it established Newman's reputation as a scholar of weight.

LEAD KINDLY LIGHT...

In 1832, Hurrell Froude was told to go to a sunnier climate for his health. And so later in the year, he, his father and Newman set off for Italy. All were steeped in Classicism and Romanticism; it was a chance to see the great ruins of Roman antiquity and a chance to explore the exotic and spectacular. For Newman, who neither liked travel nor being out of England, it was to be his 'grand tour', his gesture of exploration to the world on the other side of the English channel.

From the start there were difficulties. At Algiers he had to turn his eyes away from the sight of the French tricolour, a symbol of the victorious French revolution and the new world, which he saw as the world of irreligion and materialism. He also met Catholicism in the flesh for the first time. Up to this, Catholics and their doctrines had been met only in books; now he met it 'as a living system'. Hurrell Froude rejoiced at the ceremonies and activities he saw, but Newman was disgusted and abhorred Catholicism all the more.

In Italy Newman decided to leave the others and go off to explore the romantic wilds of Sicily alone. But there he fell ill with fever. Later he regarded this fever as a turning-point. He told his servant that he did not think he would die because he was convinced that God had chosen him for some special task. On the return journey Newman experienced a sense of divine guidance, greater than anything he himself could see and he felt that he was in the hands of a loving Providence. His mood found expression in a poem of 16 June 1833 called 'The Pillar of the Cloud', written while the orange-boat on which he was sailing from Naples to Marseilles lay becalmed between Corsica and Sardinia. We know that poem as the hymn 'Lead kindly light'.

THE OXFORD MOVEMENT
On 13 July 1833, a few days after his return home, an Oxford don whom he admired and who had influenced many of his friends, John Keble (1792–1866), preached a sermon called 'National

Apostasy'. The previous year the government had introduced the Great Reform Bill; the old established order seemed to be passing away. Just before that, Catholics had been given emancipation (1829), there had been yet another revolution in France (1830), and the forces of this un-Godly new world seemed to be winning on all sides. Now the government planned to abolish ten Anglican bishoprics in Ireland that were not needed. Keble's message was simple: Mammon was attacking God, and the Church of England was letting this happen without a fight. Now that the sky appeared to be falling, something must be done.

In the weeks that followed many believed that Keble's challenge must be taken up. The response was the Oxford Movement. The group's aims were to carry out what they saw as the reform of the Church of England, to alert it to a new awareness of its divine mission, and equip it to combat what they saw as the evils of the day. Central to their agenda was a new approach to theology and religious awareness by drawing on the Fathers of the Church, whose authority they officially acknowledged. Newman and his friends saw around them a worldly, state church in which many of their fellow Christians viewed the Gospel as just an ethical system. They wanted to change general opinion towards presenting the church as the instrument of God's will on earth.

Their method was to circulate tracts to the clergy, pointing out abuses and suggesting remedies. They called them *Tracts for the Times*; hence the group were often called 'The Tractarians', and of the ninety tracts that appeared between September 1833 and 1841, twenty-six were by Newman. He combined this work with speaking, preaching (several volumes of sermons appeared in those years), editing a journal for the movement, and writing several theological books. Much later Newman would recall this time (the mid-1830s), when he wrote on the outside of a bundle of letters thus:

March 1836 is a cardinal point of time. It gathers about it, more or less closely, the following events:
1. Froude's death.
2. My mother's death and my sister's marriage.
3. My knowing and using the Breviary.
4. First connection with the 'British Critic'.
5. The *Tracts* becoming treatises.
6. Start of the 'Library of the Fathers'.
7. Theological Society.
8. My writing against the Church of Rome.
9. Littlemore Chapel.

MEETING OPPOSITION

From the start the Tractarians were attacked as introducing Catholicism by the back-door. Initially they had no such intention and declared their abhorrence of Rome. Gradually, however, things changed. Many realised the result of the type of reform they were causing, spiritually, liturgically, and theologically, would incline them towards Catholicism, or, at the very least, would invalidate many of the reasons that were given as objections to Catholicism. Newman believed he had now found the special work God wanted of him; while at the very same time others in Oxford were now convinced that his influence had to be curtailed. It was work that combined the religious earnestness he had learned from Mayers with the rich theology he had learned from Whately, but both disapproved of the course Newman was now set upon.

Things came to a head when Newman wrote *Tract 90*, holding that the basic documents of the Church of England, known as 'The Thirty-Nine Articles', could be read in a way that was compatible with the positions taken by Rome at that time. Since the tenor of *Tract 90* was that there was little distinction between the Anglicans and Roman Catholics, it amounted to challenging the Reformation credentials of his friends and colleagues — and we must remember that in the nineteenth century it was still important to all concerned that there was 'clear water' separating

'Roman' and 'Reformed' positions. The tract provoked a storm of reaction against the movement and Newman personally. It was the end of the original movement as such. Their influence was destroyed in Oxford. Many belonging to the movement began to join the Catholic Church. Others, who still had no time for Rome, settled for some of the movement's ideas and many of its liturgical practices and formed a new grouping within the Church of England. Newman left Oxford for a quiet retreat a couple of miles away at Littlemore. Not yet ready to become a Catholic, his belief that the Church of England was 'the true Church of Christ' (a phrase he used repeatedly in his letters of this time), or at least a visible part of it, was severely shaken. Many waited to see what would happen.

LITTLEMORE

On 19 April 1842 Newman moved with a group of friends to Littlemore. There they lived like a religious order in buildings originally built as stables. A simple life-style of long walks and conversations, and prayer and study occupied the group. Every day brought news of another friend who had 'gone over to Rome'; people wanted to know what Newman would do. He was unsure; not satisfied any longer with the Church of England, he was not yet satisfied with Rome.

Things were happening, however. In September 1843 he resigned as Vicar of St Mary's. Not only did many Anglicans want to see what he would do, Catholics also were interested. In autumn 1844 Bishop Wiseman sent a recent convert, Bernard Smith, who had once been Newman's curate, to find out if it were likely Newman would become a Catholic. Smith was with him for a whole afternoon and could not raise the subject. He got his answer at dinner. He noticed that Newman was wearing grey trousers. He remembered that Newman was a stickler for correct clerical dress at all times; wearing grey trousers meant he no longer considered himself a clergyman, and so had abandoned the Church of England. He reported back that a change of course could not be far off.

The actual entry into the Catholic Church came by accident in October 1845. Dalgairns, one of the group at Littlemore who had already become a Catholic, announced that an Italian priest he knew would be staying for the night of 8 October. Newman decided he would ask that priest to receive him into the Roman Church. Newman made his final arrangements, wrote letters to all who were close to him, and prepared for his reception. As Dalgairns left to meet his friend, Newman told him his intention: 'When you see your friend, will you tell him that I wish him to receive me into the Church of Christ'. Only when the priest had arrived did he tell the group he was about to become a Catholic, and he was received later that evening.

This friend of Dalgairns who received Newman was Fr Dominic Barberi, a member of the Passionist order, who had been working for several years in England preaching parish missions and retreats. He died only a few years later (27 August 1849) in Reading, and he was declared a 'blessed' by Pope Paul VI in 1963 during the Second Vatican Council. His feastday falls on 26 August and he is referred to by his religious name: Blessed Dominic of the Mother of God.

THE DEVELOPMENT OF DOCTRINE

One of the standard criticisms made of Catholics at the time was that they had added a whole range of things (optional extras or superstitions) to the 'simple teaching of the Gospels'. If this were true, then Catholicism was false; and, if Catholicism was true, then how these developments took place had to be explained.

Newman set himself the task of explaining these developments, for if he could not explain them it would be wrong to become a Catholic. In the months before his conversion he wrote on this question in a book called *An Essay on the Development of Christian Doctrine*. His explanation was that all that is in the Church's teaching was there from the start, but the whole pattern of what

God had revealed was only visible to them after they had fully grasped the key-points of the faith. The more that the Church prayed, studied and lived, the better she was able to understand and communicate what God had done in Jesus Christ. This touched on themes that Newman had been studying in his public writings and his letters for many years. The principal theme is that one does not understand a living organism like the Church by way of fixed documents or abstract speculations, one observes the actual life of real people who have sought to follow Christ.

Development for Newman did not mean that new things were added willy-nilly to suit this or that moment, but rather that more and more aspects of a great mystery became clear in the shifting ups and downs of the Church's actual life. Just as an individual grows to know more and more about their character, their strengths and weaknesses through encountering new experiences in life, so too the practices, understanding and theology of the Church grows and changes — the continuity is not one of ideas, but of something far more precious, actual human beings, bound together to be the living body of Christ in the world through their baptism. The Church as the continuing presence of Jesus Christ is always deepening its understanding as it moves through time; seeing new ways that God is active in his world. This is the image of the church as the 'pilgrim people of God', which would play such an important role among Roman Catholics in modern theology, for example, in Vatican II. It has also meant that Newman has been continually seen as suspect by conservatives, both inside and outside Catholicism, who see Christian religion as an unchanging adherence to a set of ideas given ages ago either as a 'deposit' (the Catholic term) or as 'The Bible' (the non-Catholic term).

In contrast, Newman presented Christianity as a dynamic commitment to the living Christ by embarking on the life of faith, and this required involvement in the changes of the world and life; if faith is a living reality, then it involves change, movement, and the goal to be adhered to is not in the past, but in the future. In Littlemore, Newman realised more that ever before that Christian faith is not standing looking back at yesterday and seeking to re-create it or to remain unchanged from what once had been; rather it is to stand today, asking who one is — a process that encapsulates one's whole identity and past — and then asking about where one should go tomorrow, for it is in that direction that the destination of the Christian life lies. It was in that frame of mind that he finally asked to see Fr Barberi, and then faced the next day as a Roman Catholic.

Today we cannot appreciate the stigma that was attached to joining the Roman Catholic Church in mid-nineteenth century English society. For Newman himself, the total loss of prestige and respectability meant little. What he did miss were the friends, even relatives, who would no longer have anything but disgust for him. His letters record his sorrow; but also his consolation that he had followed his conscience. He was now in middle-age, and was, in a sense, starting again from scratch.

The following spring the group moved from Littlemore to a house provided by Bishop Wiseman near Birmingham that Newman named 'Maryvale' in honour of the Virgin Mary. There it was decided, in consultation with Wiseman, that the group would stay together and join a religious order. Wiseman felt (as did Newman himself) that the most urgent task of the day was to cope with the rising tide of atheism, and he believed that Newman was uniquely equipped for the task.

In September 1846, Newman and Ambrose St John left to study for the priesthood in Rome. There they not only got ready for ordination, but had to settle on which religious order to join. They thought of the Jesuits or the Oratorians, and settled on the latter. Pope Pius IX — then the toast of Europe as the great reforming pope — took a personal interest in Newman and the whole enterprise, so things proceeded at speed. Newman was ordained on Trinity Sunday 1847 (30 May), said his first Mass on Corpus Christi, and by 6 December had all his plans made for the Congregation of the Oratory in England and was ready to leave for home. They went by land, stopping at Loretto to place their future work under Mary's protection, and arrived in England on Christmas Eve.

In all the letters Newman wrote at this time there is one theme: the joy of being a Catholic — every day he found out some new fact or practice or detail of the Church and rejoiced over it. It was a honeymoon period. One thing, however, did not please him; he found the standard of theology in Rome on the whole poor, with an almost complete indifference to philosophy, and a leisured attitude to answering the problems of the day. Most students and teachers were resting on the laurels of the great men of the Counter Reformation, rather than setting out to do the work that urgently needed doing. Repeating famous answers by rote seemed a simpler way to the truth than confronting the awkward and difficult questions that people were actually asking, or facing the possibility that what one was relying upon was no longer good enough or downright wrong.

In 1850 it was announced by Rome that once again there would be a Catholic Hierarchy in England. This fanned anti-Catholic feelings into fire. Newman had now to defend his co-religionists. First, in 1850, he gave a series of lectures published as *The Difficulties of Anglicans*, and later in the summer of 1851 a second series now called *The Present Position of Catholics in England*. In one of these 1851 lectures he repeated the facts about a renegade Italian priest, Dr Achilli, that had been made public the previous year by Wiseman. Achilli had been in prison in the Papal States for a number of rapes and abuses of young girls. Now in England he was a celebrity, and he was whipping up anti-Catholic feelings by claiming to have escaped from the horrible dungeons of the Inquisition where he had been put, he claimed, for refusing to abandon freedom of conscience.

The English public were ready to accept that there was nothing too evil or gruesome that Rome would not stoop to, and believing that they had to destroy Rome if they would remain free, welcomed Achilli as a martyr. Achilli was dined by Palmerston, the Foreign Secretary, and fêted everywhere. When Newman brought his true past to light for the second time, Achilli charged him with slander. Despite great efforts to bring witnesses from Italy to substantiate Newman's claims, through a series of delays a conviction was achieved in June 1852.

After a further series of appeals, the situation looked hopeless and it seemed as if Newman faced a stiff prison term.

Judgement was finally given on 31 January 1853. Newman was convicted, but instead of a prison sentence he was fined £100 with £14,000 costs, the judge commenting on how Newman's morals had deteriorated since he joined forces with Roman Catholics! The delays, initially introduced to tire Newman's witnesses, did have a good effect in that they allowed tempers to cool. Meanwhile Achilli's old bad habits had begun to manifest themselves in England. The day after the judgement *The Times* magnanimously commented that the verdict and sentence was 'a great blow to the administration of justice'. The £14,000 was raised from public subscriptions.

To Dublin

In April 1851 Dr Paul Cullen, Archbishop of Armagh, asked Newman whether he would be willing to come to Dublin to run a Catholic university. Newman was excited by the project of founding a place of research and study that would form Christian laymen to live as Christians in an increasingly hostile environment. He thought of the greatness of his beloved Oxford, and imagined how much greater a Catholic university would be.

In the midst of the Achilli trial he travelled to Dublin to give the now famous opening lectures (*The Idea of a University*) and returned in February 1854 to get it started. From the outset Newman knew there were serious problems. He knew that many of the bishops, such as MacHale of Tuam, who was opposing many of Cullen's reforms, were antagonistic to the plan. However, Cullen's move from Armagh to Dublin (June 1852) made Newman believe the scheme could be carried through. As things turned out, the university never really got off the ground. There was a shortage of money and suitable staff, and a lack of interest in Ireland as a whole. Ireland, just recovering from the Famine and without the large Catholic middle class that would form the backbone of such a scheme, was not ready for this university. Likewise, the bishops, Cullen in particular, had their hands full building up parochial structures and establishing a fuller spiritual life for Catholics — it was only two decades since Emancipation. Moreover, few of the bishops, including Cullen, had any real understanding of what a university was or could do, and imagined it as a seminary for training priests. When they found that it was not doing their bidding in the way that the seminaries did, they saw it as antagonism and reacted accordingly. Newman's frustration grew and he withdrew from Dublin in 1857, disappointed that what he referred to as 'my campaign in Ireland' had produced so little.

The failure of his work in Dublin was another turning point for Newman: it marked the end of his honeymoon period as a Catholic. Newman felt particularly aggrieved by Cullen whom he saw as thwarting him, but it is probably the case that Newman never fully appreciated the complexity of the problem that Cullen faced. In the years that followed Dublin, Newman was suspected by many people (especially those influential at Rome) for his lack of orthodoxy and loyalty to the Church. At that time, when he had a very low opinion of Cullen, he did not realise that in Cullen he had one of his very few supporters whose opinion counted. Whenever asked about Newman, Cullen defended him and testified to his Catholicism. Cullen certainly recognised the greatness of Newman, and in many ways they were very similar in that both strained every fibre of his being to advance and defend the faith, but Dublin in the 1850s was not ready for Newman.

On a personal note there was another disappointment. When he first heard of the Dublin post Newman was pleased that his old mentor Whately was now the Anglican archbishop there, and looked forward to some support or friendship from him. However, despite living only a few hundred yards apart in Dublin, Whately studiously avoided meeting Newman and the two men never spoke to one another again. Newman's sense of being an isolated figure, shunned by many past acquaintances and suspected by current ones, began to grow.

THE IDEA OF A UNIVERSITY

The most enduring result of his time in Dublin was *The Idea of a University*. The lectures forming the book were given in the hall that is now the Gate Theatre. His main point was that education must not be just training in how to do this or that job, mere programming for work or material gain. Education must help the student to grow as a person and develop his or her full potential as a human being; it must train the whole person for work, for leisure, for all of life, and for death. It is an inspiring vision of education that was viewed by many then, and more since, as being uneconomic and impractical. Newman was fully aware that this would be the reaction of those who see education purely in terms of economic gain, but he was equally certain that within a Christian view of life education must be something far more. If education is only focused on economic productivity then it reduces human beings to being slaves, that is, those whose only value is their economic usefulness.

LIVING WITH ST PHILIP

In Rome in 1847, Newman and the friends who were with him decided that the life of the

Congregation of the Oratory, the religious order founded by St Philip Neri (1515–95), was the life most suited to them. From then on the practical administration of a religious house and its problems were part and parcel of Newman's life. He believed that his patron, St Philip, was particularly watching over him and often when he was surprised by a success, or a disaster that was averted, he attributed this to Philip's personal intercession.

On returning from Rome he and his friends set up their house in 'Maryvale' (1848), moved to another house nearby in the following year, and moved yet again in 1852 to Edgbaston, on the outskirts of Birmingham. From the start there were difficulties. While at 'Maryvale' they were joined by another group of converts led by Frederick Faber. Faber's group had a profound reverence for Newman but wanted to go a very different road. They wanted a far more ostentatious Catholic presence, which would declare loudly that the Roman Catholic Church was again alive in England. Newman disliked all such schemes and plans that could savour of proselytism or triumphalism. He believed that anti-Catholic prejudices were so strong that such methods would be counter-productive, bringing Catholics into disrepute. In order to avoid conflict in the Birmingham house it was decided that those who preferred the high-profile approach of Faber should go with him to found a second Oratory in London. This second Oratory was formally established on 31 May 1849.

The Birmingham Oratory continued under Newman until his death. The priests there had all the normal duties, masses, confessions, preaching, but they were constantly short of manpower and money to meet the various demands on them. Newman often noted how he had to combine his writing with the duties of bursar, librarian and sacristan. There were also special difficulties that arose from having so distinguished a superior. When Newman's loyalty was under suspicion in the 1860s, all the priests felt they had to keep away from writing and out of the public view, lest something they said or did would reflect badly on Newman. But despite all the problems the Oratory grew. By the time of Newman's death they had a vibrant community, a very successful school (founded 1859), and a country summer house at Rednal that gave much pleasure to Newman in his later years.

CLOUDS AND CONTROVERSIES

In the years that followed Dublin, Newman was a very dejected and sad figure. Project after project either came to nothing or ran into serious opposition from a group of English Catholics who were suspicious of him. Most of these Catholics who suspected that he was less than wholehearted in his Catholicism had been Anglicans and, ironically, Newman had played a major role in drawing them to Catholicism! Newman described himself as a man 'under a cloud'. He felt he had failed in Dublin. He then was asked if he would translate the Bible into contemporary English; no sooner had he started than the project folded up.

He took over editing a Catholic journal called *The Rambler*. Unfortunately many of the contributors advocated policies directly countering those then in favour at Rome, where Pius IX had changed from being an open-minded pontiff to one who took an extremely conservative position, as if the truth consisted in open warfare with the modern world. In claiming Newman as their hero contributors to the journal fuelled suspicions. Whatever Newman wrote was subjected to minute scrutiny, and those in authority who had caught the conservative tone being set in Rome were not inclined to give him the benefit of the doubt.

This period, the 1850s and '60s, was one of enormous pressure on the Catholic Church and on the papacy in particular. Italian nationalists were trying to remove the Pope as temporal ruler of regions of central Italy and those which surrounded Rome. Today we may laugh that this was considered a serious problem, but at the time many who hoped to see the papacy or Catholicism destroyed thought that getting rid of the Pope's power in Italy just might bring the whole thing to an end. In England, Cardinal Manning was one of the Pope's staunchest supporters and anyone who wanted to take a less fulsome position on the 'Roman Question' was considered of suspect loyalty, and decried for not toeing the party-line. Henry Edward Manning (1808–92) had as a young man been influenced by the Oxford Movement, indeed he wrote *Tract 78*, and had risen in the Anglican Church to become Archdeacon of Chichester. He opposed Newman's interpretation of *Tract 90* and preached a strongly anti-papal University sermon. But in 1851 he became a Catholic and quickly rose to power in his new home, becoming Archbishop of Westminster and then a cardinal.

Newman at this time was often in poor health; his letters speak of him feeling his age and his sense that death could not be far off. 'The cloud' was preventing him from getting any of those projects done that were close to his heart. He decided that he would no longer write and instead live in quiet obscurity. Though he did not know it, one of the great enemies of Catholicism was about to come to his aid.

MR KINGSLEY
The Rev. Charles Kingsley was an Anglican clergyman, a very popular novelist, and the quintessential Victorian. He was proud that he was

white, Anglo-Saxon and a Protestant, and is best remembered today as the author of the children's book, *The Water Babies*. He disliked all non-whites and believed that it was the duty of the Englishman to go out, subdue and civilise them. Prayer, peace-making and theology were not for men; he wanted a 'full-blooded religion' that carried a sword and still quoted Scripture. For many years he had felt that Catholicism (and the Jesuits in particular) were a kind of disease that sapped manly strength with theories, abstraction and piety. This became a burning hatred when he saw Catholicism making headway in England once more. Left unchecked, this would be the end of manly England, the end of her superiority and her empire. He quite rightly realised that Newman was a leading force in the introduction of this 'sissy' religion.

In January 1864 he took a new tilt at the Catholic Church, saying that Catholic priests did not really consider truth a virtue. To this he added that Newman was a prime example. Kingsley saw this evil as just one reason why he found the whole Roman system disgusting. For Newman it was the chance of a lifetime. Kingsley had made a specific charge that could be countered, and Newman, who wrote best when under pressure and with a definite need to write, was ready for him. Beginning in April, and coming out at weekly intervals until 26 May, Newman gave an entire history of how he had developed his position in the years while he was an

Anglican. He showed how at no stage had he been anything less than honest, or had any other goal than to know and do the truth. Yes, he had changed from being a virtual Calvinist when he went to Oxford to being a Catholic when he left it, but all the time these changes were motivated by the desire for the truth.

This account of his life up to 1845 is entitled *Apologia pro vita sua* (literally translated this means 'An Explanation for his Life'). It is probably the most famous autobiography in English, and second only to the *Confessions* of St Augustine among all the autobiographies yet written. The effects of the *Apologia* were many. It helped lift 'the cloud' among Catholics, but even more it gave back Newman respect among ordinary English people who had ignored him since 1845. Furthermore, apart from restoring him to general favour, it went a long way towards healing old friendships with many who had been close to him before 1845 but who had drifted away from him at that time.

It is sometimes suggested that Newman was over-sensitive to Kingsley's charges, or that he replied at such length because he wanted just such an opportunity for personal vindication. While there is a degree of truth in these statements, there was also a larger reason for the *Apologia*. To Newman, both the theological stance and the kind of religion Kingsley preached was one of the stages between a culture of faith and a culture of unbelief.

So another reason for the length and detail of his reply to Kingsley was Newman's desire to offer an alternative picture of the work of God in the lives of individuals to that which was common fare for Victorians and presented in novels like Kingsley's *Westward Ho!*. For Kingsley, religion was a rallying cry and a socio-political philosophy, for Newman it was an invitation to encounter a mystery that was far greater than the universe around us.

THE VATICAN COUNCIL (1870)

After the *Apologia* Newman's personal reputation stood higher than ever. Yet, to the group of English Catholics whom the Rome of Pius IX considered to be its most loyal supporters, Newman was still suspect. On several occasions Newman had made plans for a Catholic presence at Oxford, or at least to take pastoral care of the Catholics who were actually there, but on each occasion he was turned down.

To attempt to clear the suspicion, his long-time friend who had been with him since Littlemore, Fr Ambrose St John, was sent to Rome in 1867 to clear his name and explain any misunderstandings. He had to explain things as diverse as obscure passages in Newman's theological writing, and trivial mis-understandings such as the absence of Newman from the meal after Manning's consecration as bishop. The absence, he told them, was due to Newman's dislike of such banquets rather than a comment on Manning's theology of the papacy.

While Ambrose St John was in Rome, a new question arose: on 26 June it was announced that there would be a Council of the Church. It soon became known that, among other things, the Council would make a definition regarding the Pope's infallibility that would be binding on all Catholics. Newman was asked if he would work as a theological expert at the Council, but declined as he knew that his own lack of technical expertise in Roman-style school theology would make him subject to constant misunderstanding. Newman's only formal study of that style of theology was in the year prior to his ordination in Rome.

As the Council approached, many popular Catholic writers wrote regarding papal infallibility in a most exaggerated and incompetent way. Newman, who knew how easy it was to be side-tracked on such questions, feared that with this group so active, the Council might work with such haste that a very unsatisfactory document would be issued. This fear of haste and exaggeration, coupled with his declining the invitation to be an expert at the Council, resulted in the last cloud of Newman's life. It was suggested that he opposed the definition. In fact, Newman had accepted the infallibility of the Pope from the moment he became a Catholic and considered this belief truly part of the faith, but he questioned the practical wisdom of making it a formally defined element of faith in the religious climate of the time.

When the definition actually came, Newman had no difficulty in accepting it. The Council, despite all the pressures on them, had not accepted the exaggerated position. The Council had proposed and defined the widely accepted Catholic position. His acceptance of the Council was soon put to the test for, in 1874, William Gladstone, former Prime Minister and former disciple of the Oxford Movement, wrote against the definition of the Pope's infallibility. Newman replied in the form of a public letter addressed to the Duke of Norfolk. It was one of the last things he wrote and it expressed the Catholic teaching so well that, when someone sent it to Rome with a question-mark, it was Manning who defended him; indeed it led to a new friendship between the two men.

THE GRAMMAR OF ASSENT

All through his life Newman was struck by how easy it would be not to believe in God with certainty, i.e., to replace faith with a statement like 'there might be a God, or again there might not be, so really the whole thing is beyond us and religion is just opinions and feelings'. To tackle this growing unbelief had been his aim in his University Sermons (1826–43). On many occasions he had hoped to return and write at length on the question. But while he had touched on it, for instance in the Dublin lectures, he never had the opportunity to do much about it.

In 1866, while on holiday at Glion in Switzerland, thoughts came to him that unlocked many problems, and he began work in earnest on a book that would show how reasonable it is to have faith even though God is greater than anything we could see or touch. In the book he argued that someone can honestly believe in God, and have genuine certainty, without having gone through a whole host of investigations to see if God's existence could be proved. The human can know and confront reality, even though not everyone could then go and describe logically on paper what they are doing. He wrote up his theory of belief in a book called *The Grammar of Assent*, which appeared in March 1870. It is by far the most difficult of his writings, but has had, and continues to have, an enormous influence.

CARDINAL

In his late seventies, the love and appreciation of his friends began to be balanced by public acts of appreciation. In February 1879, his old and beloved Oxford college from his time as an undergraduate in Trinity conferred on him an Honorary Fellowship. It meant a great deal to him as it linked the Oxford Newman and the Catholic Newman once more. It signalled an end to old animosities and was a new public link with a place that was very dear to him.

In the same month Pius IX died. Newman had loved him deeply and obeyed him utterly, but held that in many practical matters and in theological tone, newer measures would have yielded better results. The new pope, Leo XIII, who had himself been 'under a cloud', albeit a smaller cloud than Newman's, promised fresh approaches.

Leo XIII had been on the 'suspect list' of those who worked in Pius IX's curia and had been sent to an out-of-the-way diocese where they hoped he could have no influence; but while there he devoted himself to the studies (mainly of the works of St Thomas Aquinas) that would form the basis of his new agenda for the church when he was elected pope. The possibility of Newman receiving some token of recognition for his work was mooted. The Duke of Norfolk mentioned the possibility of his being made a cardinal. The idea was conveyed to Leo by Cardinal Manning who endorsed it. The pope liked the suggestion, so enquiries were made as to whether Newman would accept, for Leo wanted to give him the Red Hat as a testimony to his virtues and learning, and as a formal acknowledgement that the time of suspicion was past. Newman, for his part, was delighted to receive this total vindication and endorsement of his work towards establishing a new defence of faith. Only one problem remained:

at that time, cardinals who were not bishops usually lived in Rome. Newman felt he was too old to move, so could he remain in Birmingham? Leo agreed.

It was announced on 15 March 1879, and the Red Hat was given to him in Rome on 12 May. At the ceremony Newman gave a now famous speech in which he outlined certain themes that had been his constant concern from his earliest days in Oxford:

> And I rejoice to say to one great mischief I have from the first opposed myself. For thirty, forty, fifty years I have resisted to the best of my powers the spirit of Liberalism in religion . . . [That is] the doctrine that there is no positive truth in religion, but that one creed is as good as another. . . . It is inconsistent with any recognition of any religion, as *true*. It teaches that all are to be tolerated, for all are matters of opinion. Revealed religion is not a truth, but a sentiment and a taste; not an objective fact, not miraculous; and it is the right of each individual to make it say just what strikes his fancy.

That conviction, that pursuit of truth had led him from being a Calvinist who hated all that Rome stood for, to the point when he stood in a scarlet cardinal's soutane in Rome itself.

LAST YEARS

When Newman returned from Rome he received a tumultuous welcome. For over a year he was kept busy on official engagements, receiving tributes and compliments. This was so wearing that it endangered his health. But these were not just years of gilded idleness. Newman always set great store on the importance of personal influence. Now that any 'cloud' that had been attached to him had most definitely lifted, and a new pope had come, he began to consider ways in which he might use his new position to advance the causes for which he had long worked.

Above all he desired to promote a great long-term work of apologetics that would explain and defend faith in the modern world. He even hoped, until ill-health made him abandon the idea, to go back to Rome so that he could influence his brother cardinals as to its importance. When Leo wrote his encyclical on Thomism and the importance of exploring the links of modern science with Christian philosophy, Newman wrote to the Pope expressing his enthusiasm for the project.

At last, Newman completed the task of revising and re-issuing his books; he wrote two theological essays (when aged eighty-three and eighty-four), and arranged for some of his early correspondence to be published. His interest in politics continued and his political beliefs remained unchanged. In 1832 he considered democracy an evil; and in

1885, regarding another bill to extend the right to vote, he could write to a friend: 'What a dreadful thing democracy is'.

While 'under the cloud', photographs of him show a sad and haggard face; now, despite worsening health, there is a calmness and vigour not there before. However, though receiving the Red Hat had given him a new zest for life, he could not forget that death was fast approaching. At an increasing rate he saw old friends dying and his own powers gradually diminish. He preached for the last time on 1 January 1888 and celebrated his last Mass on Christmas Day 1889. He died in Birmingham on 11 August 1890, after one day's illness, and was buried at Rednal. He had already written his epitaph: *Ex umbris et imaginibus in veritatem* ([Moving] from shadows and images towards the truth).

THE LEGACY, THE ENIGMA

In the years before he became cardinal, Newman had an awful sense that all he had attempted had failed. Today he is regarded as one of the greatest religious thinkers of the modern period and his writings are studied as religious classics. People find his writings attractive for many reasons, not least because he seems to share the modern situation with us. Newman lived in the century that saw the rise of modern non-belief and the final overthrow of the world in which it could be taken for granted that western people believed in God, both in their stated beliefs and in the way they lived. While he hardly ever refers to those who created this 'modern infidelity', everything he wrote was penned with the Christian who had to face this unbelief in mind. His stress on the importance of the Church as a spiritual reality, not just an administration — Christians are not just a group with shared beliefs, but a visible body on earth gathered by the Holy Spirit into a unity — has helped shape much of the theological thinking of the last century and lies behind many strands of modern theology. Lastly, the importance he attached to working for Christian unity, along with many hints about how problems and misunderstandings can be overcome, has been an impetus to the ecumenical movement. In his own lifetime Newman appeared to many as a man of contradictions. No one had a deeper love for the Oxford establishment, but to the people who made up that establishment he appeared for many years as a traitor to that system. As a Catholic he had a deep love of the papacy and a keen sense of its crucial importance for the Church, yet for many years he was considered someone who paid at best lip-service to it. Moreover, if one theme is constant in his thought and writings from the age of sixteen, it is his opposition to liberalism, in particular liberal theologians, and yet in his lifetime he was often suspected of liberalism by conservatives.

This enigma has continued since his death, with theologians of very different opinions claiming him as an inspiration. No doubt the complexity of Newman's character will continue to baffle those who study him, and no doubt he will continue to be used to endorse a very wide range of ideas — some indeed he would have found repulsive. Such is part of the legacy of every great thinker. Today, many pray and look forward to the time when this Oxford convert will be a canonised saint in the Roman Catholic Church; while others hold that such a move would create a distorted image of him in the minds of many who might be attracted to his writings. In that context, this enigma may illustrate a point close to Newman's heart: the Christian is drawn towards God constantly by God's love. This love draws the Christian through the darknesses, misunderstandings and difficulties of life. God reveals himself to the human heart showing the path homeward. If the Christian responds to this love and follows the pointers they discover towards the truth, then the Christian will come to meet the truth face to face. As Newman said in the 1830s: the 'Kindly Light' leads through 'the gloom, o'er the crag and torrent, till the night is gone'; and again in his epitaph: the Christian moves from shadows and reflections into the truth.

TIMELINE OF NEWMAN'S LIFE

This timeline sets out the 'before' and 'after' of events in JHN's life — it is not a complete list of his publications. Items in SMALL CAPITALS are included to sketch the context in which JHN lived.

1801   Feb. 21, born, London, eldest of six to John Newman (a banker) and Jemima Fourdrinier (of Huguenot background).

1805   Oct. 21, BATTLE OF TRAFALGAR — the adult JHN could remember the celebrations.

1808   JHN went to school in Ealing.
        BIRTH OF HENRY EDWARD MANNING.
        BIRTH OF FREDERICK WILLIAM FABER.

1809   BIRTH OF CHARLES DARWIN.

1815   June 18, THE END OF THE NAPOLEONIC WARS WITH THE BATTLE OF WATERLOO.

1816   JHN came under Evangelical influence and experienced a 'conversion'.
        Dec. 14, matriculated at Trinity College, Oxford.

1818	JHN won a Trinity scholarship of £60 p.a., tenable for nine years.
	BIRTH OF KARL MARX.
1819	JHN studied for the Bar for a short time. JHN published (with J. W. Bowden) a narrative poem entitled *St Bartholomew's Eve*.
1820	Nov., graduated B.A..
1822	April 12, JHN and E. B. Pusey elected fellows of Oriel: 'The happiest day of my life'.
1824	June 13, Trinity Sunday, ordained deacon and appointed curate of St Clements.
	Wrote 'Cicero' and 'Apollonius of Tyana' for the *Encyclopaedia Metropolitana*, and did research for Whately's book on logic.
1825	March, Vice-principal of St Alban's Hall, Oxford, under Whately.
	May 29, Pentecost, ordained priest.
	Wrote his first 'Essay on Miracles (Of Scripture)' for the *Encyclopaedia Metropolitana*.
1826	Tutor at Oriel, and was soon joined by the Catholic-minded Hurrell Froude, a pupil of John Keble.

July 2, first University Sermon ('The Philosophical Temper Enjoined by the Gospel').
R. Whately's *Logic* was published.

1827   Nov., breakdown while examining in schools.

1828   Feb. 2, made Vicar of the University Church.
Election of Edward Hawkins as provost of Oriel.

1830   JHN, Froude and Wilberforce opposed Hawkins as to the nature of a tutor's responsibilities.

1831   Whately became Anglican Archbishop of Dublin.

1831–2   JHN was one of the select 'University Preachers'.

1832   THE GREAT REFORM BILL.
JHN formally relinquished his tutorship.
Autumn, left for Italy with the Froudes.

1833   June, wrote 'Lead kindly light'.
July 14, John Keble's sermon entitled 'National Apostasy'.
Sept. 9, the first of the *Tracts for the Times*, by JHN, appeared (JHN wrote 26

of the 90 tracts): the beginning of the 'Oxford Movement'.
JHN published *The Arians of the Fourth Century*.

1834   *Lyra Apostolica* published: verses by JHN, Keble, and others.
JHN published his first volume of *Parochial and Plain Sermons*.

1835   *Parochial and Plain Sermons*, vol. 2.

1836   JHN perceived a radical change in his view of life.
Parochial and Plain Sermons, vol. 3.

1837   JHN published *The Prophetical Office of the Church reviewed relatively to Romanism and Popular Protestantism*.

1838   High-point of his influence as an Anglican.
Lectures on Justification published.
Became editor of *The British Critic*, organ of the Tractarians.
Published, with Keble, *Remains of the late Revd Richard Hurrell Froude*.

1839   JHN had his first doubts as to whether his Anglican position was tenable.
Parochial and Plain Sermons, vol. 4.

1840	*Parochial and Plain Sermons*, vol. 5.
1841	*Tract XC* published. Feb., published a series of letters in *The Times* (re-printed as the 'Tamworth Reading Room' in *Discussions and Arguments*) condemning Sir Robert Peel's remarks on science and religion made at the opening of a Reading Room at Tamworth. Manning became Archdeacon of Chichester.
1842	*Parochial and Plain Sermons*, vol. 6. Wrote his second 'Essay on Miracles (of Ecclesiastical History)' for his translation of Fleury's *Ecclesiastical History*.
1843	Resigned St Mary's; went to Littlemore. *Parochial and Plain Sermons*, vol. 7; *Sermons Preached Before the University of Oxford on Faith and Reason, 1826–1843*; and *Sermons Bearing on Subjects of the Day*.
1845	July 30, THE QUEEN'S COLLEGES BILL. Oct. 3, JHN resigned Oriel fellowship. Oct. 9, JHN joined Roman Catholic Church. Published *An Essay on the Development of Christian Doctrine*.

Nov. 17, Faber joined Roman Catholic Church.

1846   Feb. 22, JHN and companions left Littlemore.

May, JHN received 'minor orders.'

June 16, CARDINAL MASTAI-FERRETTI ELECTED POPE PIUS IX.

July, Pius IX sent JHN his special blessing.

Sept, JHN and his companions left for Rome.

1847   WORST YEAR OF FAMINE IN IRELAND. Feb., by this time a plan had been drawn up for the group to join the Oratorians.

May 30, ordained priest at Rome.

Aug. 9, Pius IX visited JHN.

Oct., A LETTER WAS SENT FROM CARDINAL FRANSONI IN ROME URGING THE IRISH BISHOPS TO SET UP A UNIVERSITY LIKE LOUVAIN.

Oct. 28, JHN began his first novel *Loss and Gain*.

Dec. 6, set out for England, arriving on Dec. 24.

1848   REVOLUTIONS IN MANY COUNTRIES ON THE CONTINENT.

Jan., the *Rambler* — a journal of Catholic thought — was founded by Frederick Capes.

Feb. 2, JHN established the Oratory at Maryvale.

JHN published *Loss and Gain: the Story of a Convert* and *Discourses addressed to Mixed Congregations*.

Oct. 11, SECOND LETTER FROM FRANSONI ON A CATHOLIC UNIVERSITY IN IRELAND.

Nov. 15, PIUS IX BESIEGED IN HIS PALACE IN ROME.

Nov. 24–25, PIUS IX FLED TO GAETA IN THE KINGDOM OF SICILY.

1849   Second Oratory in London under Faber's leadership.

JHN's Oratory moved from Maryvale.

Aug. 27, Dominic Barberi died.

1850   April 12, PIUS IX RETURNED TO ROME WITH FRENCH MILITARY SUPPORT.

April 18, THIRD LETTER FROM FRANSONI ON UNIVERSITY.

July, Wiseman detailed Achilli's immoralities in *Dublin Review*.

Aug., at the Synod of Thurles, the Irish bishops condemned the Queen's

Colleges, and announced plan for a 'Catholic University of Ireland' (C.U.I.).
Oct. 7, Wiseman announced the re-establishment of a Roman Catholic hierarchy in England and Wales. Massive anti-Catholic protests in both the streets and parliament (the Ecclesiastical Titles Act).
JHN defended the restoration in a series of lectures (published as *The Difficulties of Anglicans*); for this Pius IX granted him a DD.

1851   Feb. 21, Achilli wrote in the *Christian Times* of the need for a college in England to evangelise Italy.
April 15, Paul Cullen, then Archbishop of Armagh, wrote to JHN about a university.
Responding to anti-Catholic feeling, JHN prepared another lecture series, which began on June 30 (published as *The Present Position of Catholics in England*); on July 28 he spoke about Achilli.
Sept. 30, JHN's first visit to Ireland.
Nov. 12, JHN formally invited to become Rector.
Manning became a Roman Catholic.

| 1852 | In Dublin, on Monday afternoons (May 10, 17, 24, 31, June 7) delivered the lectures as rector-elect which grew into *The Idea of a University*.
June 21–25. Achilli trial.
June 27, returned to Ireland for Cullen's installation as Archbishop of Dublin (29th).
July 13, The new English Hierarchy meet at Oscott, JHN delivered the sermon, *The Second Spring*.
Nov. 22, JHN convicted, move for new trial. |
|---|---|
| 1853 | Jan. 31, sentenced in Achilli case.
Parochial and Plain Sermons, vol. 8. |
| 1854 | Feb. 2, JHN travelled to Ireland to start the university.
June 4, installed as Rector of C.U.I..
Nov. 3, the University, with 20 students, began work.
Letters signed 'Catholicus' (JHN) in the *Catholic Standard* on Crimean War.
Published in *Catholic University Gazette*, the *University Sketches*.
Dec. 8, PIUS IX MADE THE 'IMMACULATE CONCEPTION' AN ARTICLE OF FAITH FOR CATHOLICS.
GEORGE ELIOT PUBLISHED HER ENGLISH TRANSLATION OF |

FEUERBACH'S *THE ESSENCE OF CHRISTIANITY*.

1855   JHN published his second and last novel, *Callista, a sketch of the third century.*

1856   JHN went to Rome to sort out Oratory affairs.
        May 1, solemn opening of University Church.

1857   Aug. 26, Wiseman asked JHN to produce an English Bible, JHN accepted, but scheme fizzled out.
        Made first acquaintance with Acton.
        Published *Sermons Preached on Various Occasions*.

1858   Sept. 4 and 30, visited by Acton and Döllinger.
        Nov. 12, resigned Rectorship of C.U.I..
        Published *Lectures and Essays on University Subjects* (pt 2 of The Idea in the 1873 edn.).

1859   Jan., published 'The Benedictine Centuries' in *Atlantis*.
        March, became editor of the *Rambler*.
        May, Oratory opened a school at Edgbaston.

May 22, Bishop Ullathorne of Birmingham expressed 'wish' that he resign from the *Rambler*.

July, JHN's 'On consulting the faithful in matters of doctrine' in the *Rambler* was delated to Rome and he had to resign.

After the various disappointments, JHN ceased to publish; he felt frustrated and 'under a cloud' for several years.

DARWIN PUBLISHED *ON THE ORIGIN OF SPECIES* IN LONDON.

1860   Sept., JHN's last contribution to the *Rambler*.

1863   Death of Whately.
Death of Faber.
Charles Kingsley published *The Water Babies*.

1864   Jan., Kingsley challenged JHN's integrity in *MacMillan's Magazine*. JHN replied with the *Apologia pro vita sua* (instalments between April 21 and June 25).

After *Apologia* affair JHN planned for an Oratory at Oxford.

Aug., JHN bought land in Oxford; by Oct. the plan was in difficulties.

Nov., Manning, Ward, and others quashed the Oxford Plan.

Dec. 8, PIUS IX CONDEMNED CONTEMPORARY IDEAS IN RELIGION, PHILOSOPHY AND POLITICS BY PUBLISHING *A SYLLABUS OF ERRORS*.
Dec. 13, English Catholic bishops prohibit Catholics from attending Oxford.

1865   Jan.–Feb. 7, JHN wrote *The Dream of Gerontius* (published April–May).
Feb., death of Cardinal Wiseman; Manning succeeds him.
July, JHN resumes playing the violin.
Pusey publishes his *Eirenicon*.

1866   JHN published *Letter to Rev. E. B. Pusey on his recent Eirenicon*.
Aug., at Glion in Switzerland, discovered key for the *Grammar*.
Death of Keble.

1867   Aug. 18, plans for an Oxford house finally relinquished.
LIVING IN LONDON, MARX PUBLISHED *DAS KAPITAL* IN BERLIN.

1869   Dec. 8, opening of the Vatican Council. JHN's refusal to help with its preparations was misconstrued.

1870   March, published *A Grammar of Assent*.
JULY 18, VATICAN COUNCIL

PROCLAIMED PAPAL INFALLIBILITY.
Sept. 20, ROME SEIZED, END OF PAPAL
SECULAR RULE AND OF THE VATICAN
COUNCIL.

1871–4	JHN revised and republished his works.
1874	Gladstone wrote *The Vatican Decrees and their bearing on Civil Allegiance*.
1875	May, death of Ambrose St John. JHN replied to Gladstone in *Letter to the Duke of Norfolk*. Manning made cardinal.
1878	Feb., JHN made (first) Honorary Fellow of Trinity College Oxford. Feb. 7, DEATH OF PIUS IX; SUCCEEDED BY LEO XIII.
1879	March 15, Leo XIII announced that JHN would be made a cardinal. Aug. 4, Leo XIII published *Aeterni Patris* calling for a renewal of Christian thought.
1882	Death of Pusey. DEATH OF DARWIN IN KENT.
1883	DEATH OF MARX IN LONDON.
1884	JHN published in *Nineteenth Century*, 'On the Inspiration of Scripture'.

1885	Published in *Contemporary Review*, 'On the Development of Religious Error'.
1888	Jan. 1, JHN's last sermon.
1889	Dec. 25, JHN celebrated Mass for last time.
1890	Aug. 11, at 8.45 p.m, died at Birmingham after one day's illness, buried at Rednal.

FURTHER READING

Most of Newman's more important books (e.g. *The Essay on Development, The Idea of a University,* and the *Grammar of Assent*) are readily available both in libraries and from bookshops. However, if you are starting out on the study of Newman, then his own account of his development until 1845, the *Apologia*, is the best place to start. If you are thinking of buying any of these books, it is worth noting that they are in print both in expensive critical editions intended for scholars, and far less expensive student editions which are perfectly serviceable.

There is a wide range of readily available, modern biographies, each of which look at Newman in different ways. A good beginning — for most of the other biographies are very large — is with Owen Chadwick's *Newman* (Oxford 1983). A more extensive work, but which is both thorough and readable, is Sheridan Gilley, *Newman and His Age* (London 1990). Even more thorough, and with copious quotations from Newman's letters, is Ian Ker's *John Henry Newman* (Oxford 1988). Ker has also examined Newman as a preacher, educator, and writer in *The Achievement of John Henry Newman* (Edinburgh 1991). And books on Newman's life and work continue to appear, as witness: Vincent Ferrer Blehl, *John Henry Newman: A Pilgrim's Journey, 1801-*

1845 (London 2001). Lastly, if you are interested in Newman's period in Dublin, see Louis McRedmond, *Thrown Among Strangers* (Dublin 1990) and Donal McCartney and Thomas O'Loughlin, *Cardinal Newman: The Catholic University* (Dublin 1990).

To get an impression of Christianity in Britain in the nineteenth century, see Frances Knight, *The Nineteenth-Century and English Society* (Cambridge 1995); and for an introduction to Catholicism in Britain see J. Derek Holmes, *More Roman Than Rome: English Catholicism in the Nineteenth Century* (London 1978).

A good way of hearing of publications about Newman is through 'The Friends of Cardinal Newman' who can be contacted c/o The Oratory, Hagley Road, Birmingham B16 8UE.